THE Peruvian Vegan COOKBOOK

THE Peruvian Vegan COOKBOOK

50 easy recipes inspired by traditional Peruvian Cuisine

RECIPE ADAPTATIONS BY
Enid Soto-Lopez & Elias Lopez

PHOTOGRAPHY BY
Elias Lopez

Self published by Enid Soto-Lopez and Elias Lopez

ISBN: 978-0-578-64473-8

For details, contact hello@thedharmastore.com

A SPECIAL THANKS TO

Martha Lima and Lilia Lima

TheDharmaStore.com

Contents

Introduction

Hi there! If you got this book, you are probably following a vegan diet, or you are at least interested in plant-based cuisine. Peruvian cuisine is a true hidden gem of gastronomy, and even though ceviche is the most popular and well-known dish, there are many other great preparations that are beloved and enjoyed by Peruvian families.

Why did we make a Peruvian cookbook? Our family roots are Peruvian, and since we have been vegan for many years, we have adapted many classic Peruvian recipes so that we don't miss out on this part of our culture that is so important to us.

The richness of Peruvian cuisine has many origins, from its Inca roots to the influence of other cultures like the Spanish, Chinese, and Japanese, who have flourished for many generations in Peru. Also, Peru is a country rich in spectacular produce that is unique to the region; for example, there are over 3000 varieties of potatoes alone!

We wanted to keep the recipes as simple and traditional as possible, in fact, you don't need to know advanced cooking techniques to prepare any of the dishes, and most - if not all - of the basic equipment you will need is already in your kitchen. Some of the preparations are staples in Peruvian restaurants, but many of the dishes in this cookbook are simple and comforting family recipes that are popular in most Peruvian households.

A lot of these traditional dishes use Peruvian hot chilies as a base, but since we wanted you to be able to cook the recipes no matter where you live, we swapped most of these hard-to-get ingredients to ingredients you can find in any part of the world. There are some exceptions such as purple corn, but you can order any special ingredients online.

All the recipes in this book are mild or not spicy versions of the traditional dishes. We substituted chilies such as aji amarillo, rocoto, aji panca and aji limo for red or orange bell peppers. In Peru, you can usually order or prepare these dishes with different degrees of spiciness or even not spicy at all. In these recipes, you can add heat to your taste with cayenne pepper, white pepper, or you can use your favorite hot chilies if you are feeling adventurous.

Peruvians are really proud of their cuisine, and we are happy you will have a chance to enjoy it with these 50 Vegan Peruvian recipes we have veganized for you.

Basics

SALSA CRIOLLA

Ingredients:

1 medium red onion
2 tablespoons fresh cilantro leaves,
finely chopped
¼ cup fresh lime juice
1 teaspoon salt
White pepper to taste

Preparation:

1. Peel, wash and halve the onion, then slice it as thin as you can.
2. Put the onion slices in a bowl and season them with the salt and fresh lime juice. Also, add a pinch of pepper and mix together well.
3. In a few minutes, the onions will start to soften and "cook" in the lime juice. At this point you can adjust the seasoning to taste.
4. Finally, mix in the chopped cilantro and serve with your favorite dish.

Yields about 2 cups salsa

Note: if you want the salsa to have a less intense onion flavor, you can do the following. In a bowl, soak the sliced onions with room temperature water and a teaspoon of salt for 10 minutes. Pour the onions in a colander and rinse them well, then gently squeeze them with your hands to remove as much water as you can. You can add the salt, lime juice, pepper and cilantro after draining the onions.

CASHEW MAYO

Ingredients:

1 cup raw cashews, unsalted
½ cup water (from soaking)
1 garlic clove, roughly chopped
1 tablespoon white vinegar
1 teaspoon salt
1 teaspoon apple cider vinegar
A pinch of pepper

Preparation:

1. First, the cashews need to be soaked so that the mayo turns out softer and creamier. You can place the raw cashews in a bowl with 1 cup water and let them soak in the fridge overnight.
2. After the soaking time is complete, drain the cashews but don't discard the water. You will notice how some natural oils from the cashew remain in the liquid, so reserve ½ cup of the soaking water for the mayo preparation. You can also use ½ cup fresh water if you prefer.
3. Pour all the ingredients in a high speed blender. It helps if you pulse the ingredients first for a few times before blending. Blend until you get a smooth, glossy cream.

Yields about 1 ½ cups of cashew mayo

Note: *If you don't have time to soak the cashews, you can grab a small pot and add 2 cups water and the raw cashews. Bring them to a boil and cook on medium-high heat for 10 minutes. Let cool down and drain, then proceed with the rest of the preparation.*

Appetizers

Legend has it that this dish originated in the 19th century, when its creator used to buy potatoes in the Mantaro river valley, located in the city of Huancayo. Even though the huancaina sauce is traditionally served over boiled potatoes, many people also pour it over pasta and use it as a replacement for condiments such as mayo, ketchup and mustard.

Papa a la huancaina

ORANGE BELL PEPPER CREAM WITH POTATOES | SERVES 5

Ingredients:

FOR THE HUANCAINA CREAM:

1 orange bell pepper, cut in chunks

½ small red onion, cut in chunks

1 garlic clove, roughly chopped

¼ cup raw cashews, unsalted

1 cup almond milk

4 ounces super firm tofu, broken into chunks

2 tablespoons fresh lime juice

5 saltine crackers

2 tablespoons sunflower oil

½ teaspoon salt and a pinch of cayenne pepper

TO SERVE:

5 gold potatoes, boiled

Lettuce leaves

Peruvian botija olives* (optional)

Preparation:

1. Place a medium-sized pan on medium heat. Don't add any oil to the pan. Sauté the bell peppers and onions until they are soft and caramelized, moving the veggies constantly so that they don't burn.
2. Let the contents of the pan cool down and then transfer them to a high speed blender, and blend with the rest of the cream ingredients until you get a smooth consistency. Remember to adjust the seasoning if needed.
3. To serve, peel the boiled potatoes and cut them into 1 inch slices. Lay a few lettuce leaves on a plate and place the potato slices over the lettuce, then pour a generous amount of the cream on top of the potatoes. Decorate with a few peruvian botija olives.

Yields around 3 cups

* You can find botija olives at some hispanic grocery stores. You can also get them at amazon.com; search for "peruvian botija olives." You must get the olives that come in brine inside a jar, and not the dry kind.

This sauce comes from the southern city of Arequipa in Perú. It is said that this dish dates from the Inca times, when the messengers of the Inca empire carried a bag called "ocopa," which was filled with all the ingredients for this recipe.

Ocopa

PEANUT AND HERBS CREAM | SERVES 5

Ingredients:

FOR THE OCOPA CREAM:

¾ cup roasted unsalted peanuts
½ orange bell pepper, cut in chunks
½ red onion, cut in chunks
¼ cup fresh mint
1 tablespoon fresh basil
1 teaspoon fresh cilantro
8 small saltine crackers
1 garlic clove
1 cup almond milk
4 ounces super firm tofu, cut in chunks
2 tablespoons sunflower oil
A pinch of cumin
½ teaspoon salt and a pinch of cayenne pepper

TO SERVE:

5 gold potatoes, boiled
Lettuce leaves
Peruvian botija olives* (optional)

Preparation:

1. Place a medium-sized pan on medium heat. Don't add any oil to the pan. Sauté the bell peppers and onions until they are soft and caramelized, moving the veggies constantly so that they don't burn.

2. Let the veggies cool down and transfer to a blender, and blend with the rest of the cream ingredients. You should get a thick cream, if the cream is too runny add more saltines and check the seasoning.

3. To serve, peel the boiled potatoes and cut them into 1 inch slices. Lay a few lettuce leaves on a plate and place the potato slices over the lettuce, then pour a generous amount of the cream on top of the potatoes. Decorate with a few peruvian black olives.

Yields around 3 cups

* You can find botija olives at some hispanic grocery stores. You can also get them at amazon.com; search for "peruvian botija olives." You must get the olives that come in brine inside a jar, and not the dry kind.

Causa Rellena

LAYERED POTATO TOWER | SERVES 6

Ingredients:

FOR THE POTATO MASH:

3 pounds russet potatoes
2 large orange bell peppers, cut in chunks
¼ cup sunflower oil
½ cup lime juice
Salt and cayenne pepper
A few strips of red bell pepper and fresh parsley, to decorate

FOR THE FILLING:

One 20 ounce can of green jackfruit in brine
5 tablespoons vegan mayo
1 large ripe avocado, sliced
Salt and pepper

Preparation:

1. Wash the potatoes - do not remove the skin - and place them in a big pot with plenty of water. Boil the potatoes until tender; you can pinch them with a fork to check if they are cooked through.

2. While the potatoes are cooking, sauté the orange bell pepper chunks in a hot pan (don't add oil or seasoning) until they are soft and golden. Let the peppers cool down and transfer them to a blender, and blend them with the ¼ cup sunflower oil until you get a smooth consistency. Set this pepper cream aside.

3. When the potatoes are done, let them cool down a little and remove all the skin. I recommend you use a potato ricer if you can, because you need to mash the potatoes until they are very smooth and while they are still warm.

4. Once you get all the potatoes mashed, season them right away with the reserved pepper cream from step 2, the ½ cup lime juice and a teaspoon of salt. Proceed to mix everything together very well, using your hands to "knead" the potato mash until all the ingredients are combined. The potato mash should still feel lukewarm at this point. Check the salt, and keep kneading the potatoes until the mixture is completely smooth with no lumps.

5. For the filling, drain and squeeze the jackfruit pieces, remove all the hard parts and seeds and shred it. You should get about 1 ½ cup of shredded jackfruit. Mix the jackfruit with the vegan mayo and season with salt and pepper to taste.

6. To assemble the causa, divide the potato mixture into 2 equal parts. In a large casserole dish, place half the potatoes on the bottom, pressing down to form a smooth layer that will cover the entire base of the dish. You can use the bottom of a spoon to smooth it out.

7. Spread the jackfruit filling in an even layer over the potato base, then add the avocado slices on top.

8. Cover the filling with the remaining potato mash, making sure to press down and smooth out this last layer evenly.

9. Finally, spread a thin layer of mayo on top, and decorate with slices of red bell pepper, chopped parsley and peruvian black olives.

10. Cover and place the causa in the fridge. This dish is served cold, so make sure to have it ready at least 2 hours before eating.

Note: it is very important that you use russet potatoes; they are the closest in consistency and starchiness to the yellow potatoes used in Perú. Regarding assembling, you can also use ramekins or small bowls so that the causas are individually portioned. Just make sure to cover the container's surface with a bit of oil, or to line it with plastic wrap; this will make demolding much easier.

Causa Rellena al Olivo

LAYERED POTATO TOWER WITH OLIVE CREAM | SERVES 6

Ingredients:

FOR THE POTATO MASH:

3 pounds russet potatoes
2 large orange bell peppers, cut in chunks
¼ cup sunflower oil
½ cup lime juice
Salt and cayenne pepper

FOR THE FILLING:

16 ounces hearts of palm
10 Peruvian botija olives, seeds removed*
1 cup cashew mayo (See page 11)

* You can find botija olives at some hispanic grocery stores. You can also get them at amazon.com; search for "peruvian botija olives." You must get the olives that come in brine inside a jar, and not the dry kind.

Preparation:

1. Wash the potatoes - do not remove the skin - and place them in a big pot with plenty of water. Boil the potatoes until tender; you can pinch them with a fork to check if they are cooked through.

2. While the potatoes are cooking, sauté the orange bell pepper chunks in a hot pan (don't add oil or seasoning) until they are soft and golden. Let the peppers cool down and transfer them to a blender, and blend them with the ¼ cup sunflower oil until you get a smooth consistency. Put this pepper cream aside.

3. When the potatoes are done, let them cool down a little and remove all the skin. I recommend you use a potato ricer if you can, because you need to mash the potatoes until they are very smooth, and while they are still warm.

4. Once you get all the potatoes mashed, season them right away with the reserved pepper cream from step 2, the ½ cup lime juice and a teaspoon of salt. Proceed to mix everything together very well, using your hands to "knead" this potato mash until all the ingredients are combined. Your mash should still feel lukewarm at this point. Check the salt, and keep kneading the potatoes until the mixture is completely smooth with no lumps.

5. To prepare the olive cream, blend the cashew mayo and the olives in a high speed blender until smooth.

6. Slice the hearts of palms in ½ inch rounds, then transfer them to a bowl and toss with about 6 tablespoons of olive cream from the blender.

7. To assemble the causa, divide the potato mixture into 2 equal parts. In a large casserole dish, place half the potatoes on the bottom, pressing down to form a smooth layer that will cover the entire base of the dish. You can use the bottom of a spoon to smooth it out.

8. Spread the hearts of palm filling in an even layer over the potato base.

9. Cover the filling with the remaining potato mash, making sure to press down and smooth out this last layer evenly.

10. Finally, pour the rest of the olive cream on top of the causa.

11. Cover and place the causa in the fridge. This dish is served cold, so make sure to have it ready at least 2 hours before eating.

Note: it is very important that you use russet potatoes; they are the closest in consistency and starchiness to the yellow potatoes used in Peru. Regarding assembling, you can also use ramekins or small bowls so that the causas are individually portioned; just make sure to cover the container's surface with a bit of oil, or to line it with plastic wrap - this will make it easier to demold. Pour the olive cream on top of the causas after demolding.

Palta Rellena

STUFFED AVOCADOS | SERVES 6

Ingredients:

6 hass avocados or 3 large avocados
½ cup green jackfruit in brine, shredded
½ cup sweet peas, cooked
½ cup carrots, diced and boiled
1 small potato, diced and boiled
½ cup vegan mayo
½ cup celery, finely diced
1½ tablespoons fresh lime juice
Salt and pepper

Preparation:

1. Cut all the avocados in equally sized halves and carefully remove the pits and skin. If the holes in the center of your avocado halves are too small, scrape them off with a spoon, making sure you get an oval hole that you will later stuff with the salad.
2. To prepare the salad stuffing, mix the rest of the ingredients in a bowl and season them with the vegan mayo, lime juice and salt and pepper to taste.
3. To serve, stuff each avocado half with a few generous spoonfuls of salad. Eat right away.

Note: you can leave the skin on if you wish, just make sure to thoroughly wash the avocados before cutting them open. You can also add your favorite veggies to the salad; sweet corn and shredded cabbage are good choices.

The original version of this dish uses octopus as the main ingredient, and it was invented by a Japanese-Peruvian chef who lived in the region of Callao. The Nikkei cuisine is very popular in Perú; it is a fusion of Peruvian and Japanese cuisine originated from the great Japanese migration by the end of the 19th century.

Champiñones al olivo

PAN FRIED MUSHROOMS WITH OLIVE CREAM | SERVES 4

Ingredients:

1 pound white mushrooms, cut in ½ inch slices
3 tablespoons cooking oil
10 Peruvian botija olives*
1 cup cashew mayo (See page 11)
Salt and pepper to taste
Saltine crackers, to serve

To prepare the olive cream:

1. Remove the pits from the olives.
2. On a high speed blender, blend the cashew mayo and the olives until you get a smooth cream.

To prepare the pan fried mushrooms:

1. Place a large frying pan on high heat and add the cooking oil. When the oil is hot, drop in the mushrooms and proceed to sauté them, stirring frequently.
2. When the mushrooms start to change color and release their liquid, season them with a pinch of salt and pepper; you don't need to add much seasoning since the olive cream will provide most of the flavor in the end.
3. Continue cooking the mushrooms, moving them constantly, until they are golden and all the liquid has evaporated from the pan.

To serve:

1. Spread the mushrooms on a large serving dish and pour a generous amount of olive cream over them (you might end up with leftover cream).
2. Eat with saltine crackers, canape style.

Note: to make this a raw dish, you can replace the mushrooms with thin rounds of raw hearts of palm. You can also add avocado slices for more texture and variety.

* You can find botija olives at some hispanic grocery stores. You can also get them at amazon.com; search for "peruvian botija olives." You must get the olives that come in brine inside a jar, and not the dry kind.

Papa Rellena

STUFFED POTATO | SERVES 5

Ingredients:

FOR THE FILLING:

½ cup green lentils, uncooked
½ medium red onion, finely diced
½ red bell pepper, finely diced
2 garlic cloves, mashed
¼ cup pecans, chopped
¼ cup black raisins
½ teaspoon smoked paprika
½ teaspoon cumin
6 peruvian botija olives, pitted and chopped*
Salt and cayenne pepper
2 dry bay leaves
Vegetable oil, for cooking and frying

FOR THE POTATO DOUGH:

5 large russet potatoes
All purpose flour
Cornstarch

To make the filling:

1. Wash the lentils and place them in a pot with plenty of water; throw in the bay leaves. Bring to a boil, reduce the heat and gently simmer until the lentils are tender, making sure to add more boiling water if it gets too low.
2. Once the lentils are cooked, discard the bay leaves, and drain and reserve the lentils.
3. Grab a frying pan and add 4 tablespoons vegetable oil, then throw in the diced onions and sauté them until they start turning translucent.
4. Next, add in the mashed garlic and cook with the onions for a few minutes. Season with 1 teaspoon salt and cayenne pepper to taste. Add the diced bell pepper and sauté with the rest of the veggies until all the juices are released and evaporated, for about 5-8 minutes.
5. Now add in the cooked lentils, along with the pecans, cumin, paprika, chopped olives and raisins.
6. Mix well and taste the seasoning, add more salt and pepper to taste if needed.
7. Let this filling cook for a few minutes; you want it to be more dry than wet. When it reaches this consistency, remove from the heat and let cool.

To make the potato dough:

1. Boil the potatoes in their skins in salted water until tender.
2. Let the potatoes cool a bit and peel them, then mash them very well until you get a smooth consistency; season the mash with salt and pepper to taste.
3. If the mashed potatoes are too runny or soft, you can add a bit of flour to make them firm up. I recommend you knead this "dough" with your hands.

To make the stuffed potatoes:

1. Pour some flour on the base of a plate; you will use this to roll your assembled potatoes in the flour. In a small bowl, dilute 4 tablespoons cornstarch in 4 tablespoons of water.
2. Grab a handful of the mashed potato and using your hands, flatten it on top of your palm until you get an oval potato base that is as big or larger than your palm, and about ½ inch thick.
3. Then grab a spoonful of the lentil filling and place it in the middle of the potato base that you are holding in your hand, leaving about 1 inch space on all sides.
4. Now fold the sides inward to enclose the filling with potato; you can add more mashed potato if the top seam does not cover the filling completely. You want to shape the stuffed potato in a way similar to an american football: thick in the middle and more pointed in the ends.
5. Now proceed to roll the stuffed potato on the flour, making sure to cover its entire surface.
6. With the help of a brush, paint all the sides with the diluted cornstarch and then cover the stuffed potato in flour again. This will help it not split open when fried.
7. Repeat this process to make the rest of the stuffed potatoes. You should get about 8-10 stuffed potatoes.
8. To finish cooking them, place a small frying pan or pot on medium heat with a generous amount of vegetable oil. Wait until it is hot, then proceed to fry the stuffed potatoes (in batches) until they are golden on all sides. Serve right away with salsa criolla on top (See page 10).

Notes: you can add small cubes of tofu to the filling for some extra protein. You can also use diluted flour instead of cornstarch. For the potato dough, you can do a variation: use equal parts of cooked potatoes and cooked yuca.

* You can find botija olives at some hispanic grocery stores. You can also get them at amazon.com; search for "peruvian botija olives." You must get the olives that come in brine inside a jar, and not the dry kind. For this recipe, you can substitute the botija olives with green olives.

Mains

This is a very affordable dish for many Peruvian families because the main ingredient is a type of squash called "Macre," which is very abundant in the country. Locro is served at least once a month in Peruvian houses because it is easy, cheap and flavorful.

Locro

SQUASH STEW | SERVES 3

Ingredients:

1½ pounds winter squash or butternut squash
1 large onion, chopped
2 garlic cloves, chopped
2 large gold potatoes, peeled and cut in 1 inch cubes
½ cup sweet peas, frozen
½ cup sweet corn kernels, frozen
1 tablespoon oregano
1 tablespoon fresh mint, chopped
1 tablespoon all purpose flour
1 tablespoon sunflower oil
Salt and white pepper
½ cup cashew milk

(Optional) 4 ounces super firm tofu, cut in small cubes and soaked in ½ cup of water or unsweetened almond milk and 1 teaspoon of salt

Preparation:

1. Remove the seeds and skin from the squash, then cut it in 1 inch cubes.
2. Heat up a pot on medium heat with a tablespoon of oil and add the onions, garlic, and oregano.
3. Cook until the onions start to soften and caramelize, stirring frequently so they don't get burned. Season with salt and pepper.
4. Once the onions are cooked, add the flour and cook for a few seconds, stirring.
5. Then add the sweet peas, corn, potatoes, chopped mint and the squash cubes. Mix everything together.
6. Cover the pot and set the heat to low, and let it cook slowly until the squash is soft and the potatoes are cooked, for about 40 minutes; stir occasionally so that nothing burns or sticks to the bottom.
7. Then, add the cashew milk and tofu, and cook for 2 more minutes. Adjust the seasoning if needed. The locro should be thick and creamy, with a consistency a little runnier than a puree. Remove from the stove and serve with white rice.

Note: you can use canned peas and corn; just drain them and add them to the pot after the squash turns into puree. If you can't find fresh mint, then use an additional tablespoon of oregano instead.

Lomo Saltado is one of the most traditional dishes in Perú. It originated during the Chinese migration to Perú in the middle of the 19th century.

Lomo Saltado

STIR FRIED PORTOBELLO MUSHROOMS | SERVES 2

Ingredients:

4 large portobello mushroom caps, cut in 1 inch strips
2 roma tomatoes, cut in 1 inch wedges
1 large red onion, cut in 1 inch wedges
3 tablespoons soy sauce
1 teaspoon white vinegar
¼ teaspoon cumin
½ teaspoon oregano
White pepper
Vegetable oil, for frying

TO SERVE:

½ pound french fries, baked or fried
2 cups white rice, cooked
¼ cup parsley, chopped

Preparation:

1. This recipe cooks quickly, so have all the ingredients ready before preparation. Place a large pan or wok on medium-high heat with 1 tablespoon vegetable oil.
2. When the oil is really hot and starting to smoke, add the onions into the pan and cook, moving constantly, until they start to get caramelized but not soft.
3. Then add the tomatoes, soy sauce and vinegar into the pan. Cook for a few seconds, mixing well.
4. Now add in the mushrooms, and season everything with the oregano, cumin and a pinch of white pepper. Mix well and cook until the mushrooms start to soften, but don't let them get soggy.
5. Serve immediately and accompany with french fries and white rice. Sprinkle the chopped parsley over the mushrooms.

Note: if you can't find large portobello mushroom caps, you can use 12 ounces of baby portobello mushrooms, cut in thick slices.

Aji de Gallina

JACKFRUIT & PECAN STEW | SERVES 2

Ingredients:

Two 20 ounce cans of green jackfruit in brine
1 orange bell pepper
1 medium yellow onion, finely diced
1 garlic clove, mashed
7 small saltine crackers
¼ cup pecans
½ cup raw cashews, unsalted

1 cup almond milk, unsweetened
1 tablespoon nutritional yeast
½ teaspoon turmeric
Salt and cayenne pepper
Sunflower oil

TO SERVE:

2 medium gold potatoes, boiled
2 cups white rice, cooked

34

Preparation:

1. In a bowl, pour the almond milk and the raw cashews. Soak in the fridge overnight, or for 3-6 hours before preparing the recipe.

2. Chop the orange bell pepper in large chunks; place a frying pan on medium heat and sauté the pepper chunks until they get softer and start to brown. Remove from the heat; let them cool down a little bit and transfer to a blender. Blend with ¼ cup of water until smooth. Pour into a container and reserve.

3. In the same blender, pour the soaked cashews along with the almond milk from the bowl. Then add 7 saltine crackers (crushed), the nutritional yeast and the pecans. Blend until you get a smooth, creamy sauce.

4. Open and drain the two cans of green jackfruit. Squeeze each jackfruit piece to get rid of the excess liquid, then remove all the hard parts and seeds and shred it. You should get about 3 cup of shredded jackfruit.

5. Place a large pan on medium heat and add about 2 tablespoons of sunflower oil. Then throw the diced onions and the mashed garlic into the pan. Sauté the onions until they are soft and caramelized. Stir them frequently so they don't burn or stick to the bottom.

6. Once the onions are done, season with 1 teaspoon salt, a pinch of cayenne pepper and the turmeric; then pour the blended orange bell pepper into the pan and mix together.

7. Add the shredded jackfruit to the pan, and then incorporate the creamy pecan sauce from the blender. Lower the heat and cook for 2 more minutes, stirring frequently. Check the seasoning; add more salt and pepper if needed. This jackfruit stew needs to be creamy, almost like a thick sauce. If the stew is too dry, just add a little bit of water or almond milk to loosen it up a bit.

8. To serve, cut a boiled potato in thick slices, and lay them on a plate. Pour half the finished stew on top of the potato slices. Accompany with white rice on the side (1 cup per plate), and garnish with botija olives and fresh cilantro.

It is believed that this dish was created by Africans who arrived to Perú in the 16th century. With the passing of time, this recipe has become one of the most popular dishes in Peruvian households. This fully plant-based version is as decadent as the original!

Ceviche

MUSHROOM CEVICHE | SERVES 2

Ingredients:

1 pound white mushrooms
½ cup lime juice
2 tablespoons fresh cilantro, chopped
½ teaspoon fresh garlic, mashed
½ red onion, finely sliced
2 sweet potatoes, boiled
½ cob of corn, boiled
Salt and white pepper

Preparation:

1. Finely slice the red onion and put in a bowl. Cover it with water, add 1 teaspoon of salt and let soak.
2. Wash the mushrooms and cut them into half inch slices, and place them in a big bowl. Add the cilantro, garlic and the lime juice to the mushrooms and mix well.
3. Lastly, season with salt and white pepper, or use cayenne pepper if you want the ceviche to be more spicy.
4. Drain and rinse the onions, squeezing them a little bit to get rid of most of the water, and add them to the ceviche.
5. To serve, grab a plate, put a lettuce leaf on the bottom and place the ceviche on top. Accompany the ceviche with a few slices of boiled sweet potato and corn.

This dish appeared during the times of the Moche civilization, a culture that existed before the Inca empire; thus, ceviche is over 2000 years old. With the arrival of the Spanish conquerors, lime juice and onions were incorporated to the recipe.

Escabeche

BAKED TOFU WITH MARINATED ONIONS | SERVES 2

Ingredients:

FOR THE MARINATED ONIONS:

2 medium red onions, cut in 1 inch slices
1 red bell pepper, cut in large chunks
1 orange bell pepper, cut in large chunks
1 teaspoon smoked paprika
2 tablespoons red wine vinegar
2 tablespoons olive oil
½ teaspoon cumin
1 tablespoon oregano
Salt and cayenne pepper
2 dry bay leaves
Vegetable oil
A pinch of sugar

FOR THE BAKED TOFU:

16 ounces extra firm tofu
½ cup bread crumbs, use panko for extra crunch
2 tablespoons nutritional yeast
2 teaspoons smoked paprika
2 teaspoons dried oregano
1 teaspoon garlic powder
2½ teaspoons salt
A pinch of black pepper
2 flax eggs (2 tablespoons flax meal mixed with 2 tablespoons water)
2 teaspoons mustard
2 tablespoons olive oil

To prepare the baked tofu:

1. Preheat the oven to 400°F.
2. Drain the tofu block and pat it dry, then cut it in ½ inch slices.
3. In a bowl, mix the bread crumbs with all the dry ingredients (nutritional yeast, paprika, oregano, garlic powder, salt and black pepper).
4. In another bowl, mix the flax eggs with the mustard and olive oil. If by this time you flax eggs got too thick, add enough water to loosen them up a bit.
5. Coat all the tofu slices with the wet mixture, then cover them with the seasoned bread crumbs on all sides.
6. Lay the coated tofu slices on a lined or oiled baking tray and bake for 30 minutes, flipping them halfway, until they are golden and crispy.

To prepare the marinated onions:

1. While the tofu is in the oven, place a large frying pan on medium heat and sauté all the pepper chunks until they soften and start to brown. Remove from the heat; let the bell peppers cool down a little bit and transfer to a blender. Blend until smooth. Pour into a container and reserve.
2. Place a large pan on high heat with 2 tablespoons vegetable oil. Once the oil is hot, add the onions and sauté them quickly until they start to caramelize, for about 2-3 minutes. Take the onions out of the pan and reserve.
3. In the same pan, lower the heat to medium and add in the blended bell peppers. Once the peppers start bubbling, add in the paprika and 2 tablespoons olive oil. Cook for a few seconds, and then add in the red wine vinegar, cumin, 1½ teaspoon of salt, ½ teaspoon cayenne pepper, oregano, bay leaves, a pinch of sugar and ½ cup water. Bring everything to a gentle simmer, and then add the onions back in.
4. Mix well and let the onions cook for a few more minutes until they soften but do not break apart. Take out the bay leaves and remove the pan off the heat.
5. To serve, put 3-4 pieces of breaded tofu on each plate, and cover with half the onion escabeche. You can accompany this dish with rounds of boiled sweet potatoes, sweet corn on the cob or rice.

Notes: the marinated onions can be eaten cold. If you want, prepare them one day before serving, and store them in the fridge. You can also use mushrooms instead of tofu; just season them very lightly because the marinated onions will provide most of the flavor.

Pepián de Choclo

GREEN CORN PUREE WITH CRUNCHY TOFU | SERVES 3

Ingredients:

16 ounces extra firm tofu
16 ounces frozen sweet corn kernels, thawed
½ cup fresh cilantro, leaves and stems
5 garlic cloves, mashed
3 small red onions, finely diced
Salt and pepper to taste
Vegetable oil
3 cups white rice, cooked

FOR THE TOFU MARINADE:
¼ teaspoon garlic powder
¼ teaspoon paprika
½ teaspoon coriander powder
½ teaspoon salt
A pinch of white pepper
2 tablespoons oil

Preparation:

1. Drain the tofu and pat it dry, then cut it in 1 inch cubes. Transfer the tofu cubes to a bowl and mix with all the marinade ingredients. Let rest, preferably overnight in the fridge. Let the tofu return to room temperature before cooking it.

2. In a large frying pan, add 5 tablespoons vegetable oil, and fry the tofu on medium-high heat until it is golden and crispy on all sides. Remove the tofu cubes from the pan and place them on a dish with paper towels to absorb the excess oil.

3. Keeping the same pan hot, immediately add in the onions and garlic, and fry them until the onions are caramelized and soft, for about 15 minutes.

4. While the onions are cooking, fill a high speed blender with the corn kernels, the fresh cilantro, and a cup of water. Blend until you get a smooth consistency. Add more water if necessary to get things going; you don't want your mix to be too runny.

5. Once the onions are cooked, pour the corn cream from the blender into the pan and mix well.

6. Season with about a teaspoon of salt and a pinch of pepper (or more to taste), and let cook for 2 more minutes, stirring constantly to avoid the corn sticking to the bottom. Once the corn puree starts to bubble and slightly thicken, you can take it off the heat. The final consistency should be like a very runny potato mash.

7. Serve with a cup of white rice and fried tofu cubes sprinkled on top.

Cau Cau

POTATO & MUSHROOM STEW | SERVES 2

Ingredients:

2 pounds potatoes, boiled and cut in ½ inch cubes
16 ounces portobello mushrooms, cut in ½ inch slices
1 orange bell pepper, cut in large chunks
1 medium onion, diced
3 garlic cloves, mashed
2 tablespoons fresh mint, finely minced
1 teaspoon turmeric
¼ teaspoon cumin
1 cup almond milk
2 tablespoons fresh lime juice
Salt and pepper
Vegetable oil

Preparation:

1. Place a pan on medium heat and sauté the orange bell pepper chunks until they soften and start to brown. Remove from the heat; let the bell peppers cool down a little bit and transfer to a blender. Blend until you get a smooth paste.

2. In a large pan on medium-high heat, add 2 tablespoons vegetable oil and quickly sauté the mushrooms, seasoning them with ½ teaspoon salt, a pinch of white pepper and half of the minced mint. Cook for about 3 minutes or until the mushrooms start to sweat. Transfer the mushrooms to a container and reserve.

3. In the same pan on medium-high heat, add 1 tablespoon vegetable oil and drop in the diced onions, garlic, cumin, turmeric, the bell pepper paste from the blender, ½ teaspoon salt and a pinch of cayenne pepper.

4. Once the onions are soft, incorporate the potatoes and the almond milk to the pan. Mix well, check the seasoning, and add more salt to taste if needed.

5. When the sauce in the pan starts to simmer, throw the mushrooms back in. Then add the rest of the fresh mint and the lime juice. Mix everything well and take off the heat. Serve with white rice.

Estofado

EASY PERUVIAN STEW | SERVES 4

Ingredients:

24 oz baby portobello mushrooms, cut in large chunks
1 medium red onion, finely diced
3 garlic cloves, chopped
1 tablespoon all purpose flour
3 roma tomatoes, chopped
1 cup sweet peas, frozen
3 large carrots, thinly sliced
2 bay leaves
¼ cup raisins
½ teaspoon smoked paprika
Salt and cayenne pepper
Vegetable oil

Preparation:

1. In a large pan, heat up 2 tablespoons of vegetable oil and fry the onions, garlic and bay leaves until the onions are soft and start to golden.
2. Incorporate the flour to the pan and cook for a minute.
3. Add in the chopped tomatoes, and when they start to soften, add in the sweet peas and sliced carrots.
4. Season with the smoked paprika, 1½ teaspoons salt, and a pinch of cayenne pepper.
5. Cook for 2 minutes, then stir in the mushrooms. When the mushrooms begin to release their juices, you can add the raisins, mix everything well, and adjust the salt if needed.
6. Cook for 2 more minutes and take off the heat. Serve with rice or boiled potato chunks.

Pimientos Rellenos

STUFFED BELL PEPPERS | SERVES 5

Ingredients:

5 large red bell peppers, for stuffing
1 medium onion, finely diced
2 garlic cloves, chopped
1 cup green lentils, uncooked
½ cup white rice, uncooked
½ cup bell peppers (any color), chopped
1 teaspoon dry oregano
½ teaspoon cumin
½ teaspoon paprika
¼ cup walnuts, finely chopped
¼ cup pecans, finely chopped
5 botija olives or green olives, chopped
2 bay leaves
Salt and cayenne pepper
Vegetable oil
(Optional) vegetable stock

FOR THE BECHAMEL SAUCE:

2 tablespoons all purpose flour
2 tablespoons sunflower oil
1¼ cups almond milk
1 tablespoons nutritional yeast
¼ teaspoon garlic powder
½ teaspoon salt
A pinch of pepper

Notes: for the stuffing, if you have any leftover rice from a previous meal, you can use 1½ cups in the preparation. If you want to get canned lentils, you can use 3 cups (drained).

To make the stuffing:

1. Wash the lentils and place them in a pot with plenty of water and the bay leaves. Bring to a gentle simmer, then allow the lentils to cook until they are tender, making sure to add more boiling water if needed. Once the lentils are cooked, carefully drain them with the help of a strainer. Remove the bay leaves, and put the lentils aside. Cook the rice in your usual way and reserve.
2. In a large frying pan, add 3 tablespoons vegetable oil. Add in the ½ cup chopped bell peppers and sauté them until they start to soften. Now add in the diced onions and chopped garlic and fry them until they start to golden.
3. Season with the oregano, paprika, cumin, 1 teaspoon of salt and a pinch of cayenne pepper, and fry for a few minutes, stirring constantly.
4. Add in the cooked lentils, walnuts and pecans. Mix everything well and finally add in the chopped olives and the cooked rice. Give the stuffing a final mix to make it uniform, and take it off the heat.

To prepare the bechamel sauce:

1. In a small bowl, mix all the dry ingredients, minus the flour.
2. The almond milk needs to be warm; you can use the microwave or heat it up on low in a small pot until small bubbles start to appear on the sides.
3. Place a saucepan on medium heat and heat up the oil, then add in the flour and cook for a minute or two, stirring constantly, until the mixture starts to bubble.
4. Incorporate the heated almond milk and continue to mix the sauce. Once it starts to gently simmer, add the rest of the dry ingredients that you previously mixed in a bowl.
5. Set the heat to low and cook for a few minutes, stirring constantly, until the sauce thickens. The final consistency should be similar to a creamy potato soup. Remove from the stove when it's done.

To assemble and finish the stuffed peppers:

1. Preheat the oven to 400°F.
2. Wash the 5 red bell peppers and carefully slice the tops off each pepper (don't throw these away), then remove the core and the veins with the help of a spoon. Rinse the peppers again to remove any leftover seeds.
3. In a deep roasting pan, drizzle some oil at the bottom and add in ½ cup water or vegetable stock. Stuff each bell pepper with the lentil mixture, very tightly packed from the bottom and all the way to the top, then cover it with a pepper top. Lay all the stuffed bell peppers in the roasting pan.
4. Pour the cheesy bechamel sauce over the stuffed peppers, and bake them in the oven for around 45-50 minutes or until the peppers are tender and golden.

Coliflor Saltada

STIR FRIED CAULIFLOWER | SERVES 4

Ingredients:

1 cauliflower head
1 medium red onion, cut in 1 inch slices
1 red bell pepper, cut in strips
2 roma tomatoes, cut in 1 inch slices
½ cup fresh parsley, chopped

½ pound french fries, frozen
⅓ cup soy sauce
1 teaspoon white vinegar
Vegetable oil
Salt and pepper

Preparation:

1. Cook the french fries and set them aside.
2. Break the cauliflower head into florets, then cut each floret into ½ inch slices. Steam the cauliflower slices until al dente. You can also boil them in salted water, but make sure they do not get mushy. Drain if necessary, and let cool down.
3. In a large wok or frying pan, add 4 tablespoons vegetable oil and sauté the bell peppers on high heat for around 30 seconds. Add the onions and sauté them for another 30 seconds.
4. Add the steamed cauliflower to the pan and cook with the rest of the veggies for 2 minutes, then add in the tomatoes.
5. Season everything with the soy sauce, vinegar and a pinch of pepper, mixing well so that all the veggies get coated with the sauce.
6. Once the tomatoes start to soften a little, incorporate the french fries into the pan. Mix well and cook for a minute to allow the fries to absorb some of the juice.
7. Taste the cauliflower and add a little bit of salt if needed. You do not want any of the veggies to get mushy, so remove the pan from the heat as soon as you are happy with the seasoning.
8. To finish, sprinkle the chopped parsley on top. Serve with white rice.

Notes: if you prefer, you can make your own french fries for this recipe. Just wash and cut 2 large potatoes into wedges, lightly salt them and fry them in hot oil until golden. You can use cilantro instead of parsley to finish off the dish.

Frejoles con Seco

BEANS WITH MUSHROOM STEW | SERVES 4

Ingredients:

FOR THE MUSHROOM STEW:

12 ounces baby portobello mushrooms, chopped in 1 inch pieces
1 medium red onion, finely diced
5 garlic cloves, mashed
1 red bell pepper, cut in chunks
1 orange bell pepper, cut in chunks
1 red bell pepper, cut in strips
1 cup fresh cilantro (or use culantro if you can find it)
½ cup sweet peas, frozen
1 large carrot, sliced in rounds
1 tablespoon oregano
1 teaspoon cumin
1 cup beer
Vegetable oil
Salt and pepper

FOR THE BEANS:

Two 15 ounce cans of great northern beans or pinto beans
1 medium red onion, finely diced
1 large roma tomato, diced
1 teaspoon paprika
1 teaspoon cumin
Vegetable oil
Salt

TO SERVE:

4 cups white rice, cooked

To prepare the mushroom stew:

1. Bring a small pot of salted water to a boil. Pour in the sweet peas and carrots, and cook until they are tender, for about 10 minutes. Drain and reserve.
2. Place a pan on medium heat and sauté all the red and orange bell pepper chunks until they soften and start to brown. Let the bell peppers cool down a little bit, then transfer them to a high speed blender and blend until you get a smooth, runny paste. Pour into a container and reserve.
3. In the blender, add all the fresh cilantro (or culantro) along with ½ cup water, and blend on high until you get a runny paste.
4. Put a large frying pan on medium heat with 4 tablespoons vegetable oil and pour in 1 cup of diced onions. Once the onions turn translucent, add in the garlic and let everything cook until the garlic starts to golden.
5. Add in the bell pepper paste, and cook for about 8 minutes, until the mixture thickens and all the liquid is evaporated.
6. Now add in the cilantro paste from the blender, and cook for 10 more minutes until the sauce is reduced again. Season with the cumin and oregano.
7. At this point, pour the cup of beer and the red bell pepper strips into the pan. Simmer for about 5 minutes to let the alcohol evaporate, then drop in the portobello mushrooms.
8. Season with 1 teaspoon salt or to taste; give everything a good mix and cook for about 5 more minutes or until the mushrooms are tender.
9. Mix in the boiled sweet peas and carrots, and remove the pan from the heat.

To prepare the beans:

1. Drain the canned beans. In a bowl, drop the contents of one of the cans and add ½ cup water; mash the beans with the help of a fork. You can also do this using a food processor; just a few pulses will work.
2. Place a pot on medium heat with 3 tablespoons vegetable oil, and pour in the rest of the diced onions. Cook them until they turn soft and caramelize, then add in the mashed garlic and cook for 2 minutes.
3. Now add in the diced tomato, and mix frequently until the veggies reduce. Season with the cumin, paprika, 1 teaspoon salt and a pinch of pepper.
4. Add the mashed beans from the bowl and the can of whole beans to the pot, and mix well. Let simmer for 2-3 minutes and remove from the heat.

To serve:

Put a serving of rice on each plate and a few spoonfuls of beans next to the rice. Spoon in the mushroom stew on top of the beans.

In Perú, it is very popular to eat lentils on Mondays. There is a belief that if you eat them that day you will attract good luck and money to your home.

Lentejas de la casa

HOMESTYLE LENTILS | SERVES 4

Ingredients:

1 cup green lentils, uncooked
1 medium onion, finely diced
4 garlic cloves, mashed
2 roma tomatoes, deseeded and diced
1 medium potato, boiled and cut into ½ inch cubes
1 teaspoon cumin
1 teaspoon smoked paprika
2 bay leaves
Salt and pepper
Vegetable oil

Preparation:

1. Wash the lentils and place them with the bay leaves in a pot with plenty of water. Bring to a boil, reduce the heat and gently simmer until the lentils are tender, making sure to add more boiling water if it gets too low. Once the lentils are cooked, discard the bay leaves, and drain and reserve the lentils.
2. Place a large pan on medium-high heat with 4 tablespoons vegetable oil. Throw the diced onions into the pan and sauté them until they are reduced and caramelized, then add in the mashed garlic and cook for a minute.
3. Incorporate the diced tomatoes and let cook, stirring occasionally, until all the juices in the pan are reduced.
4. Season with the cumin, paprika, pepper to taste and 1 teaspoon salt; mix well and proceed to incorporate the lentils and the boiled potato cubes.
5. If the lentils are too dry, you can add a splash of water to loosen them up. Mix everything very well and let cook for 2 more minutes; taste the seasoning and add more if needed.
6. Serve the lentils with rice.

Guiso

JACKFRUIT & POTATO STEW | SERVES 2

Ingredients:

Two 20 ounce cans of green jackfruit in brine
3 potatoes, cut in ½ inch cubes
1 red bell pepper, cut in strips
1 medium yellow onion, diced
5 garlic cloves, mashed
1 teaspoon paprika
1 teaspoon cumin
2 tablespoons tomato paste
Vegetable oil
Salt and pepper

Preparation:

1. Drain and squeeze the jackfruit pieces, remove all the hard parts and seeds and shred it. You should get about 3 cups of shredded jackfruit. Place in a bowl and reserve.

2. In a large frying pan on medium-high heat, add 4 tablespoons vegetable oil. Throw in the mashed garlic and let cook for a minute, then incorporate the diced onions.

3. Once the onions start to get translucent, season with the paprika, cumin, tomato paste, 1 teaspoon salt and a pinch of pepper.

4. Mix well and fry for a couple of minutes, then add in the red bell pepper strips and cook for another minute.

5. Add the diced potatoes to the pan, along with about 1½ cups water (or enough to cover the veggies half way), and add an extra teaspoon of salt.

6. When the liquid starts to simmer, lower the heat to medium and cover the pan with a lid. After about 15 minutes, the potatoes should be tender when pinched with a fork.

7. At this point, add in the shredded jackfruit and mix well. Let cook for 5 minutes; the stew should be juicy but not too soupy. Remove from the stove and serve with white rice.

Quinoa is a Peruvian superfood. The Incas said it was a sacred food, which they offered to the Sun God in a gold plate. Quinoa was also used for medicinal purposes.

Quinoa Atamalada

CREAMY QUINOA | SERVES 3

Ingredients:

1 cup white quinoa, uncooked
1 medium red onion, very finely diced
4 garlic cloves, mashed
1 orange bell pepper, cut in chunks
1 large potato, boiled and cut in medium cubes
½ cup raw cashews, unsalted

1 tablespoon nutritional yeast
1 teaspoon smoked paprika
1 teaspoon cumin
1 teaspoon oregano
Salt and cayenne pepper
Vegetable oil

Preparation:

1. Wash the quinoa very thoroughly and place it in a pot with 2 cups water or vegetable broth, and a pinch of salt. Bring it to a boil, cover and lower the heat so it cooks with a gentle simmer for 10-15 minutes. When it's done, the quinoa will turn translucent and its white germ will show. Reserve.

2. While the quinoa is cooking, place a frying pan on medium heat and sauté the orange pepper chunks until they soften and start to brown. Remove from the heat; let the bell peppers cool down a little bit and transfer to a blender. Blend until smooth. Pour in a container and reserve.

3. Place the raw cashews in a small pot with 1 cup water; bring to a boil and let cook for 4 minutes. Cool down and transfer to a blender. Blend until you get a smooth, runny cream.

4. In a large frying pan, add 4 tablespoons of vegetable oil and throw in the onions. When the onions turn translucent, add the mashed garlic and sauté until everything starts to golden.

5. Now add in the blended bell pepper paste and the paprika, cumin, oregano, 1 tsp salt, and cayenne pepper to taste.

6. Let everything fry for about 5 minutes until all the liquids in the pan are reduced and the veggies start to form a paste.

7. Add the cooked quinoa to the pan and 1 cup water. When the water starts to simmer, add the nutritional yeast and the cashew cream from the blender. Return to a simmer and add in the cooked potato cubes. Adjust the seasoning and take off the heat.

Rice & Pasta

Frejoles Castilla

BLACK EYED PEAS WITH RICE | SERVES 4

Ingredients:

1 cup black eyed peas, soaked overnight

1 cup rice, uncooked and rinsed

1 orange bell pepper, cut in chunks

1 red bell pepper, cut in chunks

1 red onion, diced

5 garlic cloves, mashed

1 teaspoon cumin

1 teaspoon paprika

1 tablespoon oregano

2 bay leaves

Vegetable oil

Salt and white pepper

Preparation:

1. With the help of a large strainer, wash the black eyed peas that have been soaking overnight, and place them in a large pot with plenty of water and the bay leaves. Bring to a boil, then lower the heat and allow the black eye peas to simmer, covered with a lid. Check after 40 minutes to see if they are cooked; add more boiling water if the peas are not covered and need more time to cook. When they are done, they will be tender but not mushy. Drain the black eyed peas, take out the bay leaves and reserve.

2. Place a large pot on medium heat and sauté all the bell pepper chunks until they soften and start to brown. Remove from the heat; let the bell peppers cool down a little bit and transfer to a blender. Blend until smooth.

3. Return your large pot to medium-high heat, then add 5 tablespoons vegetable oil and the diced onions. When the onions start turning translucent, add the mashed garlic and fry for a few seconds.

4. Then mix in the cumin, paprika, oregano, ¼ teaspoon pepper, and after a few seconds, add the bell pepper paste from the blender.

5. Let everything cook for a few minutes until a thick paste starts to form, then add in the cooked black eyed peas and 2½ cups water.

6. When the water in the pot starts to bubble, add in the uncooked rice and season with 1 tablespoon salt (or to taste). Cover the pot with a lid and set the heat to medium-low.

7. Cook for 15-20 minutes until all the water is evaporated and the rice is al dente. Remove from the stove and let rest, covered, for 5 minutes before serving.

8. You can sprinkle chopped fresh cilantro on top when serving, or you can also top it with freshly made salsa criolla (See page 10).

Note: if all the water evaporates but the rice is still undercooked, just add an extra ¼ to ½ cups water (the amount will depend on how gritty the rice is), and keep cooking it covered on low heat until the rice is done.

This is a very family-oriented dish that is rarely found in restaurants.

Tallarines Verdes

NOODLES IN GREEN SAUCE | SERVES 3

Ingredients:

1 pound of pasta of your choice
Vegetable oil

FOR THE GREEN SAUCE:

5 ounces fresh baby spinach
3 ounces fresh basil
3 garlic cloves, roughly chopped
1 small onion, roughly chopped
⅓ cup pecans
4 ounces extra firm tofu, cut in chunks
⅓ cup almond milk
½ teaspoons garlic powder
2 tablespoons nutritional yeast
1 tablespoon fresh lime juice
1 tablespoon olive oil
1½ teaspoons salt

FOR THE BAKED TOFU:

16 ounces extra firm tofu
½ cup bread crumbs
2 tablespoons nutritional yeast
2 teaspoons smoked paprika
2 teaspoons dried oregano
1 teaspoon garlic powder
2½ teaspoons salt
A pinch of black pepper
2 flax eggs (2 tablespoons flax meal mixed with 2 tablespoons water)
2 teaspoons mustard
2 tablespoons olive oil

To prepare the baked tofu:

1. Preheat the oven to 400°F.
2. Drain the tofu block and pat it dry, then cut it in ½ inch slices.
3. In a bowl, mix the bread crumbs with all the dry ingredients (nutritional yeast, paprika, oregano, garlic powder, salt and black pepper).
4. In another bowl, mix the flax eggs with the mustard and olive oil. If by this time you flax eggs got very thick, add enough water to loosen them up a bit.
5. Coat all the tofu slices with the wet mixture, then cover them with the seasoned bread crumbs on all sides.
6. Lay the coated tofu slices on a lined or oiled baking tray and bake for 30 minutes, flipping them halfway, until they are golden and crispy.

To prepare the green sauce:

1. While the tofu is in the oven, cook the pasta until al dente according to the instructions on the package.
2. Place a large pan on medium-high heat with 4 tablespoons vegetable oil. Sauté the onions and garlic until the onions start to soften.
3. Add the spinach and half of the basil to the pan, and cook until the leaves just start to wilt. Transfer the contents of the pan to a blender, and blend with the leftover fresh basil and all the remaining sauce ingredients.
4. You can slowly add in more almond milk if needed to help loosen up the sauce in the blender. Once you get a smooth consistency, return the sauce to the pan.
5. Set the heat to low and cook the sauce for a few minutes until it starts to bubble and thicken a bit. Then add your cooked pasta to the pan and mix together very well, making sure to coat each noodle with the sauce.
6. Serve on a plate with 2 or 3 slices of baked tofu on top of the pasta. You can also accompany this dish with papa a la huancaina (See page 14).

Note: *you can add in more lime juice and nutritional yeast to the sauce for more intense flavors. For a creamier sauce, you can replace the tofu with ½ cup raw cashews, soaked overnight and drained. You can also top off your finished pasta with cooked green beans or steamed carrots.*

This dish takes inspiration from the traditional pesto sauce, which became popular after Italian immigrants arrived to Perú.

Tacu Tacu

CRUNCHY RICE WITH REFRIED BEANS | SERVES 3

Ingredients:

2 cups diced onions

1 large orange bell pepper, cut in chunks

5 garlic cloves, mashed

3 cups cooked white rice

Two 15 ounce cans of pinto beans

1 teaspoon dry oregano

½ teaspoon cumin

Salt and cayenne pepper

Vegetable oil

Salsa criolla (See page 10)

When African slaves were brought to Perú, they created this dish using leftovers they received from other meals. The name "Tacu Tacu" comes from the Quechua word "Tacuni," which means to mix one thing with another.

To prepare the refried beans:

1. Place a frying pan on medium heat and sauté the orange bell pepper chunks until they soften and start to brown. Remove from the heat; let the bell peppers cool down a little bit and transfer to a blender. Blend until smooth; pour into a container and reserve.
2. Drain and wash the pinto beans, then put half of the beans along with ½ cup water in the blender and blend until you get a cream.
3. Put a large frying pan on medium-high heat with 4 tablespoons vegetable oil. Add 1 cup of the diced onions and half the garlic. Sauté this mix until the onions start to soften and caramelize, then add in the oregano, cumin, 1 teaspoon salt and a pinch of cayenne pepper. (Optional: add a splash of vinegar of your choice to make the flavors pop).
4. Now incorporate the blended bell peppers and cook for one minute, then add in the bean cream from the blender and the rest of the pinto beans.
5. Mix everything well and add readjust the seasoning if needed. Cook for two more minutes and remove from the stove. The consistency of the finished beans should be like a very thick soup or cream.

To prepare the tacu tacu:

1. This recipe yields 3 servings. You will prepare each of the servings one at a time.
2. Set a small non-stick frying pan on high heat, add 2-3 tablespoons vegetable oil and a third of the remaining onions and garlic.
3. Sauté for about 2 minutes to let the onions soften, then add in a cup of cooked rice and a third of the prepared beans. Mix well.
4. With the help of a spatula, shape the rice and bean mixture into an oval in the middle of the pan.
5. Let it fry for a few minutes and start turning it with the spatula so that it retains an oval shape that you can roll in the pan. The idea is that the rice and bean mixture fries and browns all around to form a crunchy crust, while remaining soft on the inside. Don't worry if your shape is not perfect or if it crumbles a bit when turning it; the only thing that matters is that you get those delicious crispy bits of rice and beans in your plate.
6. When the tacu tacu is golden on all sides, transfer it to a plate and then proceed to prepare the remaining 2 portions.
7. Top each finished serving with a spoonful of salsa criolla before eating.

Arroz Tapado

COVERED RICE TOWER | SERVES 4

Ingredients:

2 cups rice, uncooked

1 cup green lentils, uncooked

1 small onion, finely diced

1 green bell pepper, diced

2 roma tomatoes, diced

1 garlic clove, mashed

¼ cup raisins

8 botija olives*, pitted and chopped

2 bay leaves

1 tablespoon balsamic vinegar

1 teaspoon paprika

1 teaspoon oregano

Salt and pepper

Vegetable oil

Chopped parsley, to decorate

Preparation:

1. Cook the rice al dente according to the instructions on the package of your preferred brand.
2. Wash the lentils and place them with the bay leaves in a pot with plenty of water. Bring to a boil, reduce the heat and gently simmer until the lentils are tender, making sure to add more boiling water if it gets too low. Once the lentils are cooked, discard the bay leaves, and drain and reserve the lentils.
3. Place a large frying pan on medium-high heat with 4 tablespoons vegetable oil. When the oil is hot, sauté the diced bell peppers for about 10 minutes or until they are golden.
4. Add the onions, garlic and oregano to the pan, and cook until the onions are soft. Season with the balsamic vinegar, paprika, a teaspoon of salt and a pinch of pepper.
5. Add in the cooked lentils and raisins. Taste the seasoning and adjust if needed. Cook for a few minutes and take off the heat, then mix in the diced tomatoes and chopped olives.

To serve:

1. Divide the rice and lentils into 4 equal parts, one for each plate. Each serving will be assembled one at a time.
2. Grab a small bowl and grease its walls with a bit of oil. Spoon in half of a portion of rice at the bottom of the bowl and press it down to form an even layer.
3. Spoon in one portion of the lentil preparation on top of the rice, pressing it down and smoothing it out with the bottom of the spoon.
4. Cover the lentils with the remaining half portion of rice. Make sure the rice is tightly pressed and even.
5. Place a plate over the bowl and flip it upside down to release the rice "tower" on the plate.
6. Repeat this process for the remaining servings of rice and lentils.
7. Decorate with chopped parsley on top.

Note: if the rice is sticking to the bowl and you have a hard time demolding the rice tower, you can line the bowl with plastic wrap before assembling.

* You can find botija olives at some hispanic grocery stores. You can also get them at amazon.com; search for "peruvian botija olives." You must get the olives that come in brine inside a jar, and not the dry kind. For this recipe, you can substitute the botija olives with green olives.

Arroz con pollo

GREEN RICE | SERVES 4

Ingredients:

3 cups jasmine rice, uncooked
1 medium onion, diced
½ cup carrots, diced
½ cup sweet corn, frozen
½ cup green peas, frozen
1½ cup bell peppers (any color), diced
3 garlic cloves, chopped

½ cup fresh cilantro
½ cup baby spinach
¼ cup beer
1 teaspoon paprika
Salt and pepper
Vegetable oil

Preparation:

1. This recipe cooks quickly, so make sure you rinse the rice and have all the ingredients ready beforehand.
2. In a high speed blender, add the cilantro and spinach with ⅓ cup water, and blend until you get a smooth, runny paste.
3. Put a large pot on medium-high heat with 5 tablespoons vegetable oil; when the oil is hot incorporate the onions, bell peppers and garlic. Cook until the onions and peppers are soft.
4. Add in the beer and the cilantro and spinach paste from the blender to the pot. Incorporate the carrots, sweet corn, green peas and rice.
5. Let everything fry for a few minutes, constantly stirring it so the rice doesn't stick to the bottom.
6. Season with the paprika, 1 tablespoon of salt and a pinch of cayenne pepper. Mix well.
7. Pour 4½ cups of water into the pot (or the amount you use to get al dente rice; this can vary depending on the altitude of the place you live in).
8. Let the rice boil on medium-high for about 10 minutes. It's important you don't let the rice completely dry up, so stay close to check how much liquid is left.
9. Once the water is almost evaporated, set the heat to low, cover the pot and let the steam finish cooking the rice for about 15 more minutes or until the rice is al dente.
10. Fluff with a fork and serve right away.

This very popular dish originated with the arrival of Chinese immigrants to Perú. The name "Chaufa" comes from the chinese "Chaufan," which means "fried rice."

Arroz Chaufa

PERUVIAN FRIED RICE | SERVES 3

Ingredients:

2 cups jasmine rice, uncooked
1 cup green onions, chopped, white parts set aside
1 cup red bell peppers, diced
3 garlic cloves, mashed
1 inch chunk of fresh ginger, cut in small pieces
½ cup soy sauce
2 teaspoons sugar
1 teaspoon sesame oil
Vegetable oil

Preparation:

1. A day before preparing the recipe, cook the rice al dente with no salt, and according to the instructions on the package of your preferred brand. Refrigerate.
2. In a large wok or frying pan, heat up 5 tablespoons vegetable oil on high heat and drop in the garlic, ginger and the white parts of the green onions.
3. Cook for one minute, then add in the bell peppers and cook until they start getting soft. Add the sugar.
4. Incorporate a third of the rice, mix well, and continue adding rice until all of it is in the pan.
5. Add the soy sauce and sesame oil, and mix everything until the rice is uniform in color.
6. Turn off the heat and incorporate the rest of the green onions. Serve immediately.

Notes: it's ok if you use freshly prepared rice for this dish, but the resulting texture could be a bit mushy; letting the rice cool off and rest overnight allows the grains to fry better and remain al dente. You can add any other vegetables you like: carrots, broccoli and onions are great options. You can use low sodium soy sauce or less than the amount in the recipe if your soy sauce is too salty. You can sprinkle toasted sesame seeds on top of the rice when serving.

Tallarín Saltado

PERUVIAN STIR FRIED NOODLES | SERVES 2

Ingredients:

14 ounces chinese yellow noodles, wheat based

1 tablespoon garlic, mashed

1 tablespoon fresh ginger, grated

1 red bell pepper, cut in strips

½ cup green onion stalks (white parts), cut in 1 inch sticks

2 ounces snow peas, cut in chunks

3 baby bok choys, cut in chunks

10 napa cabbage leaves, cut in chunks

1 cup carrots, sliced

1 tablespoon cornstarch, dissolved in 3 tablespoons water

1 cup green onions (green parts), finely sliced

Sesame oil

Vegetable oil

For the stir fry sauce:

½ cup soy sauce

1 tablespoon rice vinegar

1½ tablespoons sugar

1 teaspoon sesame oil

A pinch of cayenne pepper

Preparation:

1. Fill a large pot with water; add one tablespoon of salt and around 2 tablespoons vegetable oil and bring to a boil.

2. Cook the noodles in boiling water until al dente, following the instructions on the package. If the noodles come with no instructions, check them after 3 minutes because they usually cook very quickly.

3. Drain the noodles with the help of a colander, then return them to the pot and season them with 2 tablespoons sesame oil. Set aside.

4. Combine all the stir fry sauce ingredients in a bowl and reserve.

5. Grab a large frying pan or wok and add 5 tablespoons vegetable oil; throw in the garlic and ginger and cook on high heat for a few seconds, moving constantly to avoid burning.

6. Then add in the red bell pepper strips, green onion stalks and snow peas. Let cook for a minute, and then add the bok choy, napa cabbage and carrots.

7. Once the cabbage starts to wilt, add the stir fry sauce to the pan. When the liquid in the pan starts to simmer, add in the dissolved cornstarch and cook until the sauce starts to thicken. Don't let the sauce dry too much; add a splash of water to loosen it up if needed.

8. Remove the sauce from the heat and pour it over the noodles. Add the sliced green onions to the pot and mix everything very well. Serve immediately.

Notes: you can find the noodles in asian supermarkets, just make sure they are made of wheat and colored with turmeric. If you use low sodium soy sauce, you might need to add more, or a pinch of salt, to taste. You can adjust the seasoning once the noodles and stir fried veggies are combined. You can also use other veggies for the stir fry: bean sprouts, broccoli florets and mushroom slices are other traditional choices.

Arroz con Aceitunas

BLACK OLIVE RICE | SERVES 3

Ingredients:

2 cups jasmine rice, uncooked

1 medium red onion, finely diced

1 orange bell pepper, cut in chunks

1 cup botija olives*

3 garlic cloves, mashed

½ cup black raisins

½ cup pecans, chopped

½ teaspoon cumin

Salt and white pepper

Olive oil

Preparation:

1. Place a frying pan on medium heat and sauté the orange bell pepper chunks until they soften and start to brown. Remove from the heat; let the bell peppers cool down a little bit and transfer to a blender. Blend until smooth. Pour into a container and reserve.

2. Cook the rice al dente with a pinch of salt, and according to the instructions on the package of your preferred brand. Set aside.

3. Remove the pits from the olives and transfer them to a blender with ¼ cup water. Blend until you get a smooth cream.

4. On a large frying pan, add 5 tablespoons olive oil and the diced onions, and sauté until the onions turn translucent.

5. Add the garlic and cook until it starts to golden, then pour the blended orange bell pepper into the pan. Season with the cumin, 1 teaspoon salt and a pinch of white pepper. Cook until all the liquid evaporates.

6. Add the olive cream to the pan, along with the raisins and pecans, and mix well. When the sauce starts bubbling, set the heat to low.

7. Spoon in the cooked rice into the pan and carefully fold it into the sauce until all the grains are uniformly covered. Serve right away.

You can find botija olives at some hispanic grocery stores. You can also get them at amazon.com; search for "peruvian botija olives." You must get the olives that come in brine inside a jar, and not the dry kind.

Arroz a la Jardinera

GARDEN RICE | SERVES 3

Ingredients:

2 cups jasmine rice, uncooked

1 orange bell pepper, cut in chunks

1 large red onion, finely diced

3 garlic cloves, mashed

1 cup sweet peas, frozen

1 cup carrots, diced

1 cup sweet corn, frozen

1 red bell pepper, cut in strips

1 teaspoon cumin

1 tablespoon dry oregano

1 teaspoon turmeric

½ teaspoon paprika

1 teaspoon red wine vinegar

Salt and pepper

Vegetable oil

Preparation:

1. Place a frying pan on medium heat and sauté the orange bell pepper chunks until they soften and start to brown. Remove from the heat; let the bell peppers cool down a little bit and transfer to a blender. Blend until smooth.

2. Place a large pot on high heat with 5 tablespoons vegetable oil. Add the onions and fry them until translucent, then add in the garlic and cumin. Cook until the garlic starts to turn gold, then add in the orange bell pepper from the blender.

3. Season with the turmeric and paprika. Cook for a minute, then add in the red wine vinegar, oregano and a pinch of pepper. Mix well.

4. Incorporate the rice to the pot and fry it for a minute; you want to get it a bit toasted while it's still raw. Add in 3¼ cups* water (or stock), the sweet peas, carrots, sweet corn, and red bell pepper strips. Season with a tablespoon of salt or more to taste. You can check the seasosing by tasting a bit of the cooking water; it needs to be as salty as a soup.

5. Cook, uncovered on high heat. Once the water is almost evaporated (when you move the rice you can see the bottom of the pan), turn the heat to low and cover the pot with a lid. The rice will finish cooking with steam, for about 8-10 more minutes. Remove from the stove when the rice is al dente. Serve warm.

*If you live in a place with higher elevation, you will need to use more liquid. You can use the amount you normally use to make your rice al dente, plus an additional ¼ cup.

Street Food

This sandwich is typically prepared on Sundays by restaurants, street vendors and also at homes. It is part of the popular "criollo" breakfast.

Pan con Chicharrón

CRISPY TOFU SANDWICH | SERVES 4

Ingredients:

4 small bread buns, use ciabatta
3 small sweet potatoes, cut in ¼ inch slices
1 cup of salsa criolla (See page 10)
Vegetable oil

FOR THE MARINATED TOFU:

8 ounces of super firm tofu, cut into ¼ inch slices
⅓ cup soy sauce
½ teaspoon cumin
1 teaspoon paprika
1 teaspoon white vinegar
A pinch of white pepper

Preparation:

1. In a container, mix all the marinade ingredients, then add the tofu slices and let marinade in the fridge for as long as you can, best if overnight.
2. Heat up or toast the bread buns in the oven while you prepare the rest of the recipe. Make sure you have the salsa criolla ready.
3. Add plenty of oil to a frying pan on medium-high heat, then fry the marinated tofu slices until they are golden and crispy on all sides. Line a plate with paper towels to remove excess oil from the slices as you take them off the pan.
4. Then on the same pan, fry the sweet potato slices until they are golden on both sides; drain them on paper towels too.
5. Cut the bread buns in half. Add a layer of sweet potatoes on the bottom, then a layer of crispy tofu on top, and finally top them off with a spoonful of salsa criolla.

Makes 4 sandwiches

The traditional version of this sandwich is a "must" for sandwich shops and street vendors. It is also very popular for birthdays, where they are served as sliders.

Sandwich de pollo

JACKFRUIT SANDWICH | SERVES 4

Ingredients:

Two 20 ounce cans of green jackfruit in brine
2 stalks of celery, finely diced
4 small bread buns, use ciabatta or hamburger buns
4 leaves of butter lettuce
5 tablespoons vegan mayo
Shoestring potatoes
Salt and pepper

Preparation:

1. Heat up or lightly toast the bread buns in the oven while you prepare the rest of the recipe.
2. Open and drain the two cans of green jackfruit. Squeeze each jackfruit piece to get rid of the excess liquid, then remove all the hard parts and seeds and shred it; place the shredded jackfruit in a bowl. You should get about 3 cup of shredded jackfruit.
3. Add the celery to the bowl and season everything with the vegan mayo, salt and pepper to taste.
4. Cut the bread buns in half. Place a lettuce leaf on the bottom, then spoon in the jackfruit mix, sprinkle some shoestring potatoes on top and then close each bun.

Makes 4 sandwiches

Triple Clásico

CLASSIC TRI-LAYERED SANDWICH | SERVES 2

Ingredients:

4 ounces extra firm tofu, cut in small cubes
1 roma tomato, sliced
1 hass avocado, sliced
8 slices of classic sandwich bread
Vegan mayo
½ teaspoon mustard
Salt and pepper

Preparation:

1. In a bowl, place the cubes of tofu and season them with the mustard, 3 tablespoons vegan mayo and salt and pepper to taste.
2. The recipe makes 2 sandwiches; you will need 4 slices of bread, and half the tomato and avocado for each sandwich.
3. Grab a bread slice and spread half of the seasoned tofu evenly, then cover with a second slice of bread. Spread a thin layer of vegan mayo over the top of the bread slice, then add a layer of tomato slices; season the tomatoes with a sprinkle of salt.
4. Grab another slice of bread and spread a thin layer of mayo on one side. Cover the tomato layer with this bread slice, with the mayo side facing the tomatoes.
5. Then spread a thin layer of mayo on top of the bread, and add a layer of avocado slices. Sprinkle the avocado slices with salt to taste.
6. Grab the last slice of bread and spread a very thin layer of mayo on one side, then cover the avocado layer with this bread, the mayo side facing the avocado.
7. Cut in half diagonally, and serve right away.

Makes 2 sandwiches

Triple de Aceituna

TRI-LAYERED SANDWICH WITH OLIVES | SERVES 2

Ingredients:

4 ounces extra firm tofu, cut in small cubes
12 botija olives,* pitted and chopped
1 hass avocado, sliced
8 slices of classic sandwich bread
Vegan mayo
½ teaspoon mustard
Salt and pepper

Preparation:

1. In a bowl, place the cubes of tofu and season them with the mustard, 3 tablespoons vegan mayo and salt and pepper to taste.
2. The recipe makes 2 sandwiches; you will need 4 slices of bread, and half the olives and avocado slices for each sandwich.
3. Grab a bread slice and spread a thin layer of vegan mayo on one side, then cover it with an even layer of chopped olives.
4. Grab the second slice of bread and spread a thin layer of mayo on it, then cover the olive layer, mayo side facing the olives.
5. Spread a thin layer of mayo on the top side of the bread and proceed to add a layer of avocado slices, which you will then sprinkle with salt to taste.
6. Grab the third bread slice and spread a thin layer of mayo on it, then cover the avocados with the mayo side facing down.
7. Add half of the seasoned tofu on top of the bread, in an even layer. Cover the tofu with the remaining bread slice. Cut in half diagonally, and serve right away.

Makes 2 sandwiches

* You can find botija olives at some hispanic grocery stores. You can also get them at amazon.com; search for "peruvian botija olives." You must get the olives that come in brine inside a jar, and not the dry kind.

Anticuchos

MARINATED VEGGIE SKEWERS | SERVES 3

Ingredients:

8 ounces baby portobello mushrooms, stalks removed
1 large red bell pepper, cut in chunks
1 large red onion, cut in chunks
3 wood skewers

FOR THE MARINADE:

3 garlic cloves, mashed
1 teaspoon cumin
1 teaspoon oregano
¼ teaspoon cayenne pepper
2 tablespoons balsamic vinegar
1 red bell pepper
1 tablespoon salt

SIDES:

2 ears of corn, quartered and boiled in salted water
2 potatoes, boiled and cut in 1 inch slices

To prepare the marinade:

1. Cut the red bell pepper in large chunks. Place a skillet on medium-high heat and sauté the bell pepper until it starts softening and caramelizing.
2. Take off the heat and let cool, then transfer the chunks to a high speed blender and blend until you get a smooth, runny paste.
3. Pour the bell pepper paste in a bowl and mix with the rest of the marinade ingredients.

To prepare the skewers:

1. Stick the veggies in the skewers in an alternating sequence: you can add bell pepper chunks followed by a mushroom cap and a few onion chunks.
2. Repeat until all the skewers are full, then lay them on a deep dish and pour the marinade over the skewers, making sure it covers all sides.
3. Place the skewers in the fridge for 1-2 hours or overnight (covered) to allow the vegetables to marinade before cooking.

To cook the skewers:

1. You can use a griddle or a grill; if using the griddle, coat the bottom in cooking oil and cook the skewers on medium heat to allow the veggies to soften without getting burned.
2. Spoon any leftover marinade over the skewers as they cook so they are infused with more flavor. Make sure to turn them every few minutes so that all the sides cook evenly.
3. Once the veggies are gold and tender, they are ready.
4. Serve the veggie skewers with potato slices and corn on the cob.

Note: you can use other veggies for the skewers; zucchini and cherry tomatoes are great alternatives.

"Salchipapa" is one of the most popular street foods in Perú because of its low cost. The base of the dish is always hot dogs and potatoes, but there are many variations for the sauces and dips that go with it.

Salchipapas

VEGGIE HOT DOG & POTATO MEDLEY | SERVES 4

Ingredients:

1½ pounds baby potatoes
1 pack of vegan hot dogs (6-8 links)
Olive oil
Dry oregano
Salt and pepper

FOR THE CRIOLLA MAYO:

Half of a medium red onion, finely sliced
3 tablespoons fresh lime juice
5 sprigs of fresh cilantro, leaves and stalks
½ cup raw cashews, soaked overnight
1 garlic clove
1 tablespoon white vinegar

Preparation:

1. Wash and cut the baby potatoes in half, then soak them in cold water for 20 minutes. Preheat the oven to 450°F.
2. Drain and dry the potatoes with paper towels, then lay them on a baking tray and toss them with olive oil, salt and oregano to taste. Roast for about 20-25 minutes until the potatoes are golden on the outside and fork tender on the inside.
3. While the potatoes are roasting, prepare the criolla mayo. In a small bowl, mix the sliced red onions with the lime juice, a teaspoon of salt and a sprinkle of white pepper. Let marinade for 10-15 minutes, until the onions turn soft and release some of their natural juices.
4. Grab a high speed blender and pour the marinated onions (juice and all), an extra ½ teaspoon salt and the rest of the criolla mayo ingredients, and blend until you get a smooth and creamy consistency.
5. Slice the hot dogs into ½ inch rounds, then place a large frying pan with a generous amount of oil on medium-high heat and fry the hot dog rounds until golden.
6. To serve, combine the roasted potatoes and the hot dogs in a large serving plate and drizzle some of the criolla mayo on top. You can also put the mayo on the side in a small bowl as a dip.

Note: you can replace the roasted potatoes for traditional french fries. Instead of the criolla mayo, you can also use plain vegan mayo, ketchup or mustard.

Soups

Crema de Zapallo

SQUASH CREAM | SERVES 4

Ingredients:

2 pounds winter squash or butternut squash

½ cup raw cashews, unsalted

1 medium onion, finely diced

3 garlic cloves, finely chopped

1 tablespoon nutritional yeast

1 cup almond milk

1½ tablespoons fresh lime juice

Salt and pepper

Vegetable oil

Preparation:

1. To prepare the squash for cooking, take the skin off, scrape off the seeds with a spoon and rinse the squash with water. Cut the clean squash into large cubes.

2. In a large pot, place the squash and raw cashews with 4½ cups water and cook on medium heat until the squash is very tender.

3. In a high speed blender, spoon in the cooked squash and cashews until the blender is almost full, then add one cup of the cooking liquid from the pot. Blend until you get a smooth cream, and pour it into a large container. You will probably need to do this in batches, so keep repeating this step until all the squash and cashews are blended. If you run out of cooking water, you can use tap water or almond milk. If you have leftover cooking water after everything is blended, take it out of the pot and reserve it just in case the cream gets too thick later on.

4. Return the empty pot to medium-high heat and sauté the onions and garlic with 2 tablespoons vegetable oil until the onions are reduced and caramelized.

5. Set the heat to low and add the squash cream back into the pot. Season with the nutritional yeast, 2½ teaspoons salt and a pinch of pepper.

6. Add in the almond milk and let the cream simmer for a few minutes. When it is done, remove from the stove and incorporate the lime juice. Give the cream a last whirl and serve.

Note: to thicken the cream, you can substitute the cashews with one tablespoon all purpose flour: mix it in when the onions are almost done caramelizing and cook it for a minute before you pour in the blended squash.

Crema de Espinaca

SPINACH CREAM | SERVES 4

Ingredients:

10 ounces baby spinach
1 tablespoon all purpose flour
½ cup raw unsalted cashews, soaked overnight
3 cups vegetable stock
2 cups almond milk
Salt and pepper
Olive oil

Preparation:

1. Place a large pot on medium heat and sauté the spinach until it wilts.
2. Transfer the spinach to a blender, and blend with the raw cashews and a cup of stock until smooth.
3. Put the pot back on the stove on medium heat, and add 2 tablespoons olive oil and the flour.
4. When the flour starts to bubble, add the almond milk and the rest of the vegetable stock.
5. Bring to a boil and cook for about 3 minutes. Incorporate the blended spinach cream from the blender, and season with salt and pepper to taste.
6. Stir frequently for about 5 minutes or until the cream starts to thicken. Serve right away.

Notes: *if you forget to soak the cashews overnight, you can boil them on high heat for about 5 minutes. Let cool and drain. When the cream is finished, you can squeeze in some lime juice to brighten up the flavors.*

If you ever visit the city of Lima in Perú and you party until very late, you will find many places selling this soup. It is a popular cure for hangovers, so many people also call it "levanta muertos" (wake the dead).

Aguadito

CHUNKY GARDEN SOUP | SERVES 2

Ingredients:

1 orange bell pepper, cut in chunks

2 cups fresh cilantro, leaves and stalks

1 medium red onion, finely diced

5 garlic cloves, mashed

1 cup sweet peas, frozen

1 cup sweet corn, frozen

1 red bell pepper, cut in strips

2 large potatoes, boiled and cut in chunks

2 cups cooked white rice

½ teaspoon cumin

1 teaspoon dry oregano

Salt and pepper

Vegetable oil

(Optional) Fresh lime juice

Preparation:

1. Place a frying pan on medium heat and sauté the orange bell pepper chunks until they soften and start to brown. Remove from the heat; let the bell peppers cool down a little bit and transfer to a blender. Blend until smooth. Pour into a container and reserve.

2. Place all the fresh cilantro in the blender and blend with ½ cup water until you get a smooth consistency. You can add a bit more water to help get things moving, if needed.

3. Place a large pot on medium-high heat with 5 tablespoons vegetable oil. When the oil is hot, add the diced onions and fry them for a few minutes until translucent, then add the garlic and cook for 2 minutes.

4. Add the blended orange bell pepper to the pot and cook until the mixture thickens and starts to caramelize, for about 10 minutes.

5. Add the cilantro paste from the blender and 4½ cups water to the pot, and season the soup with the cumin, oregano, a tablespoon of salt and ¼ teaspoon of pepper (or more to taste).

6. When the soup breaks into a boil, add in the sweet peas and corn and let simmer for 5 minutes.

7. Add the red bell pepper strips, the potato chunks and the cooked rice to the soup, and let cook for 7 more minutes. Serve immediately, as the soup thickens with time. Sprinkle a few drops of lime juice on your bowl to add some brightness.

Sopa de garbanzos

CHICKPEAS SOUP | SERVES 4

Ingredients:

Two 16 oz cans cooked chickpeas

8 cups of vegetable stock

1 tomato, diced

1 red onion, diced

1 carrot, finely sliced

2 cups fresh baby spinach

2 garlic cloves, minced

1 cup of cooked rice

1 tablespoon tomato paste

1 teaspoon smoked paprika

1 tablespoon dried oregano

3 tablespoons vegetable oil

Salt and pepper

Preparation:

1. Place a pot on medium-high heat and add the vegetable oil, diced onions, oregano and garlic. Cook, stirring frequently, until the onions are caramelized.

2. Add the sliced carrots, diced tomatoes, paprika and tomato paste to the pot and cook for a few minutes.

3. Pour the chickpeas and the 8 cups of vegetable stock into the pot. Bring to a boil and let simmer, uncovered, for 10-15 minutes until the soup is reduced. Season with salt and pepper to taste.

4. Finally, incorporate the cooked rice and fresh spinach to the pot and turn off the heat.

Notes: The texture of the chickpeas you get will affect the thickness of the soup. If you want a creamier soup, just blend half a can of chickpeas with a cup of water in a high speed blender. If you want to cook your own chickpeas from scratch, you will need about 1 Lb for this recipe. Cook them in plenty of unsalted water until they are tender and creamy when squeezed between your fingers, and then wash and drain them before proceeding with the recipe.

Sweets

Pastel de Choclo

CORN CAKE | SERVES 6

Ingredients:

1 pound sweet corn, frozen

½ cup almond milk

1 teaspoon anise seeds

¼ cup raisins

½ cup raw cane sugar

½ teaspoon ground cinnamon

1 tablespoon sunflower oil

1 teaspoon vanilla essence

¾ cups all purpose flour

Preparation:

1. Preheat the oven to 350°F.
2. Allow the sweet corn to thaw, then transfer it to a blender and blend with the almond milk until you get a thick cream. Pour into a small mixing bowl.
3. Add in the anise seeds, raisins, sugar, cinnamon, sunflower oil, and the vanilla essence. Mix well.
4. Using a fine-mesh strainer, gradually sift the flour into the bowl while mixing the batter at the same time; this will help avoid any lumps in the batter.
5. Grease the inside of a small baking dish, then pour the batter in and smooth it out evenly.
6. Bake for about 50 minutes or until a toothpick comes out clean from the middle of the cake, and the top is golden brown.

Notes: if the raw batter is too runny, the cake will take longer to cook in the oven. When the cake is done, the toothpick may have some sticky residue, but it should not be wet like the batter.

Arroz con Leche

RICE PUDDING | SERVES 4

Ingredients:

1 cup jasmine rice, uncooked and thoroughly washed
3 cups almond milk
1 cinnamon stick
5 cloves
½ cup raisins
1 cup coconut milk
¼ cup maple syrup
1 teaspoon vanilla extract
Cinnamon powder, to serve

Preparation:

1. In a medium pot, pour the almond milk, and drop in the cinnamon stick and cloves.
2. Add the rice into the pot. When the milk starts to simmer, set the heat to low, cover the pot with a lid and cook for about 10 minutes or until all the liquid is almost completely absorbed. Stir frequently to make sure the rice does not stick to the bottom.
3. Now remove the lid from the pot and add the coconut milk, maple syrup, vanilla extract and raisins. Mix well and let cook for 1 more minute; the rice should be creamy and a bit runny. If it is too dry, you can add more almond milk.
4. Remove the pot from the stove and transfer its contents to a bowl. You can serve it lukewarm, or let it chill in the fridge.
5. When serving, sprinkle cinnamon powder on top.

Notes: *this dessert is also served combined with mazamorra morada (page 112).*

Chicha Morada

PURPLE CORN JUICE

Ingredients:

FOR THE PURPLE CORN ESSENCE:

15 ounces purple corn ears*

12 cups water

The peel and core of one pineapple

The peel of one apple

10 cloves

2 cinnamon sticks

1 teaspoon anise seeds

FOR THE PURPLE CORN JUICE:

Sugar

Fresh lime juice

You can find dry purple corn ears at amazon.com if you search for "maiz morado" or purple corn. You want to get the ears, not just the kernels.

To prepare the purple corn essence:

1. Strip the kernels from the purple corn cobs, and place them in a large colander, along with the bare cobs; rinse them thoroughly.
2. Place the kernels and bare cobs in a large pot with the rest of the ingredients for the essence.
3. Set the heat to medium-high, and bring to a boil.
4. Let boil vigorously for 45 minutes; you will start to see how the skin of the kernels will start cracking a bit. At this point you can remove the pot from the stove and let the contents cool down a little.
5. With the help of a big slotted spoon, remove the bigger pieces from the concentrate: peels, cobs, cinnamon sticks, kernels.
6. Then grab a fine mesh colander and place a big bowl or container underneath, and proceed to strain the concentrate from the pot until only the liquid remains in your bowl.
7. This dark and spiced liquid will be the base for this drink. This is also a key ingredient in another recipe called "mazamorra morada," which is a very traditional dessert; you can find the recipe on page 112.

This recipe makes around 6 cups of purple corn essence or concentrate.

To prepare the purple corn juice:

1. Mix an equal part of purple corn concentrate with an equal part of water. The amount of sugar and lime depends on how much chicha you want to make.
2. For a 64 ounce pitcher, you can use the juice of 3-4 limes and around ½ cup sugar to sweeten.
3. You can also prepare it by the glass: use 2 tablespoons fresh lime juice and 2-3 tablespoons of sugar. You can add more or less sugar depending on your personal taste.

Chicha morada is the most popular drink in Perú; you can find it in most restaurant menus and it is sold by many street vendors. Purple corn was used by the Inca empire in ritual ceremonies and also for medicinal purposes.

Arroz Zambito

GOLDEN SPICED RICE | SERVES 4

Ingredients:

1 cup jasmine rice, uncooked
1½ cups coconut milk
8 ounces panela (raw cane sugar brick) or dry evaporated cane juice
1 cinnamon stick
3 cloves
½ cup black raisins
½ cup chopped pecans
Cinnamon powder, to serve

Preparation:

1. Wash the rice and place it in a pot with 2 cups water (or use ½ cup more of the amount of water you normally use when cooking rice) and cook until the rice is very tender; you want it a bit overcooked. Remove from the heat and reserve.

2. On a separate pot, pour the coconut milk, panela (cut in chunks), cinnamon stick and cloves. Bring to a gentle simmer on medium-low heat. Don't set the heat on high or the contents of the pot will overflow.

3. Simmer until all the panela has dissolved, for about 8-10 minutes; then remove from the heat and take out the cloves and cinnamon stick.

4. Bring the pot of rice back to the stove on medium heat, and pour the spiced milk on top of the rice. Mix well, and once it starts simmering, incorporate the raisins and chopped pecans.

5. Cook until the liquid starts reducing but the rice is still creamy and a little wet, for 2-3 more minutes. Remove from the stove.

6. To serve, add a few spoonfuls of rice in a small serving bowl and sprinkle with powdered cinnamon and chopped pecans.

Notes: you can substitute the coconut milk for any other plant-based milk of your preference. You can use walnuts instead of pecans. You can also sprinkle grated coconut on top when serving. You can eat this dish lukewarm or let it chill in the fridge.

Mazamorra Morada

PURPLE CORN PUDDING | SERVES 4

Ingredients:

2 cups purple corn essence (See page 108)
¼ cup fresh pineapple, diced
¼ cup fresh apples, peeled and diced
¼ cup fresh peaches, peeled and diced
4 dry apricots, chopped
4 dry prunes, chopped
¼ cup raw cane sugar
¼ cup cornstarch, dissolved in ¼ cup water (at room temperature)
1½ tablespoons fresh lime juice

Preparation:

1. In a medium sized pot, add the diced pineapple, apple, peaches, apricots and prunes with 1 cup water; set the heat on the stove to medium and when the water starts to simmer, add in the sugar and let everything cook for 5 minutes. This will help soften the fruits and release their flavor.
2. Next, add in the purple corn essence. When you get a gentle simmer, slowly add in the dissolved cornstarch to the pot (give it a quick whisk first in case some starch settled in the bottom) and mix constantly for 1 minute; you will notice how the liquid will thicken very quickly. At this point you can taste and add more sugar if you want.
3. Finally, add the lime juice, mix well and remove from the stove. Serve lukewarm with sprinkled cinnamon powder on top.

Notes: the traditional recipe uses potato starch, sweet potato starch or a mix of both instead of cornstarch. You can use those if you can find them; just make sure to slowly drizzle in the starch (previously dissolved in water) and stop adding it when the liquid thickens. This dessert is also served combined with arroz con leche (page 106).

Dulce de camote

SWEET POTATO SLICES IN CARAMEL SAUCE | SERVES 3

Ingredients:

1½ pounds sweet potato

1 orange

3 cinnamon sticks

9 cloves

1 cup raw cane sugar

Preparation:

1. Peel the sweet potatoes, then wash them and cut them in ½ inch slices.
2. You will use the peel and the juice of the orange for this recipe. To make sure the peel is free of waxes or dirt, you can wash it with non-toxic soap (the one used specially to clean produce). Cut the orange in half and squeeze the juice from it, and scrape all the leftover pulp inside so that you end up with just the peels. Reserve the juice and slice the orange peels in roughly 1 inch slices.
3. In a medium pot, pour ⅓ of the sugar at the bottom, then cover it with a layer of ⅓ of the sweet potato slices. Add 3 cloves and a few pieces of the cinnamon sticks; you can carefully snap the sticks with your hands so that you have smaller pieces to add to the pot. Add ⅓ of the orange peel slices.
4. Keep adding the remaining ingredients in the same order to make 2 more layers.
5. You will need to pour 1 cup of liquid inside the pot. Grab the reserved orange juice and measure this amount; you can complete the cup with water if you don't have enough orange juice.
6. Place the pot on low heat, cover, and cook for about 35 minutes or until the sweet potato is fork tender and the liquid has turned into a syrup. This spiced caramel sauce will coat the sweet potatoes and can also be poured over them. Serve warm.

Side Dishes

Ensalada Rusa Peruana

PERUVIAN RUSSIAN SALAD | SERVES 4

Ingredients:

2 medium beetroots

2 medium potatoes

3 large carrots

½ cup sweet peas, frozen

½ cup green beans, chopped in ½ inch pieces

¾ cups cashew mayo (See page 11) or vegan mayo

3 tablespoons fresh lime juice

Salt and pepper

Preparation:

1. Fill a large pot with water and boil the beets, potatoes and carrots until fork tender. These roots have different cook times: the carrots will be done first, then the potatoes, and the beets will probably need to cook for much longer. Keep a pot of boiling water on the side in case you need to refill the big pot to help finish cooking the beets.
2. After all the vegetables are cooked, drain them, remove them from the pot and let them cool down.
3. In a smaller pot, put salted water to a boil and cook the snow peas and green beans until tender, for about 10 minutes. Drain and let cool.
4. Peel the skin off the beets, potatoes and carrots and cut them into ½ inch cubes, placing them in a big bowl as you go. Then add in the snow peas and green beans to the bowl.
5. Season the salad with the mayo, lime juice, salt and pepper to taste.
6. Mix everything well and adjust the seasoning to your taste; you can add more mayo if you want more creaminess and more lime if you want bolder flavors. Serve chilled.

Torrejas

VEGGIE CAKES | SERVES 6

Ingredients:

Half a cauliflower head

1 small yellow onion, diced

½ cup finely grated carrots

½ cup fresh parsley, chopped

½ cup green onions, chopped

1 cup all purpose flour

Salt and pepper

Vegetable oil

Preparation:

1. Cut the cauliflower into florets and boil them in salted water until they are very tender, then drain and let cool down. Chop the cooked cauliflower into very small pieces; you will need 2 cups for this recipe.
2. Place a large frying pan on medium heat with 2 tablespoons vegetable oil; add the diced yellow onions and a pinch of salt and sauté them until they turn soft and translucent.
3. Grab a large bowl and combine all the rest of the vegetables together. Add the cauliflower and onions you cooked in the previous step.
4. In another bowl, add a cup of water, 1½ teaspoons salt, and ¼ teaspoon pepper (or more if you want more heat). Slowly incorporate the flour to the bowl, constantly whisking it with a fork until you get a thick but smooth batter.
5. Pour the batter into the veggies and mix well. You will need to cook the veggie cakes in batches. This mixture yields about 12-14 veggie cakes (depending on how big your spoonfuls are).
6. Return the frying pan to medium heat with a good amount of vegetable oil (enough for frying). When the oil is hot, scoop out a big spoonful of mixture and place it on the pan, flattening it with the bottom of the spoon to form a patty of about ½ inch thickness.
7. Add as many cakes to the pan as you can comfortably fit, leaving space in between so you can easily move them around. Let them turn gold on one side, and then with the help of a spatula, flip them over to cook on the other side.
8. When the veggie cakes are golden all over, remove them from the pan and place them on a plate lined with paper towels to absorb the excess oil. Serve right away.

Notes: you can use other veggies you like; sweet corn, green peas and bell peppers are great alternatives. The cauliflower is a very important binder for this recipe, but a good replacement (though not traditional) is also a rustic mash of boiled potatoes. You can also bake the cakes instead of frying them; add 2 tablespoons oil to the veggie batter, line the patties on a baking tray and bake at 400°F until golden.

Yields around 12–14 veggie cakes

Pastel de Papa

POTATO & LENTIL PIE | SERVES 6

Ingredients:

2½ pounds gold potatoes

1 cup green lentils, uncooked

1 medium yellow onion, diced

5 garlic cloves, minced

2 roma tomatoes, diced

⅓ cup black raisins

⅓ cup pecans, chopped

12 green olives, sliced

½ cup fresh parsley, finely chopped

1 teaspoon paprika

1 teaspoon cumin

2 bay leaves

Salt and black pepper

Vegetable oil

Preparation:

1. Wash the lentils and place them with the bay leaves in a pot with plenty of water. Bring to a boil, reduce the heat and gently simmer until the lentils are tender, making sure to add more boiling water if it gets too low. Once the lentils are cooked, discard the bay leaves, and drain and reserve the lentils.

2. Peel, quarter and boil the potatoes in salted water until fork tender. Drain and mash the potatoes until smooth; season them with salt and pepper to taste. You can add a bit of oil or vegan butter to make the mash more creamy and soft.

3. Place a large frying pan on medium-high heat with 5 tablespoons vegetable oil. Add the diced onions to the pan and fry them until caramelized, then add in the garlic and cook for 2 minutes.

4. Add the diced tomatoes to the pan; once they start softening, incorporate the paprika, cumin, 2 teaspoons salt and pepper to taste.

5. Mix and let cook for 2 minutes, then add in the cooked lentils, raisins and pecans. If the mix is too dry, add in ⅓ cup water.

6. Cook for a minute, mixing well, then add in the sliced olives. Finally, incorporate the parsley, adjust the seasoning if needed and remove from the stove.

7. Preheat the oven to 425°F.

8. Grab a baking dish and add half of the mashed potatoes on the bottom in an even layer, then pour the lentils on top and level with a spoon. Finally, cover the lentils with an even layer of the remaining potato mash. Drizzle with olive oil and bake for 25 minutes or until golden.

Pastel de Coliflor

CREAMY CAULIFLOWER CASSEROLE | SERVES 6

Ingredients:

1 large cauliflower head

FOR THE CASHEW CREAM:

½ cup raw cashews, unsalted
1 tablespoon white vinegar
1 garlic clove
½ teaspoon salt

FOR THE CHEESY SAUCE:

3 tablespoons all purpose flour
1 cup almond milk, warmed
½ teaspoon garlic powder
¼ teaspoon grated nutmeg
2 tablespoons nutritional yeast
Salt and cayenne pepper
Vegetable oil

Preparation:

Cut the cauliflower into florets, then boil in salted water until very tender. Drain, let cool a bit and crush until you get a chunky cauliflower mash. Season with 1 teaspoon salt (or to taste).

To prepare the cheesy sauce:

1. Place a small pot on medium-low heat, and add 3 tablespoons vegetable oil and the flour.
2. Dissolve the flour in the oil and slowly cook, stirring constantly, until it starts to bubble. Then slowly add in the warm almond milk, stirring constantly to get a uniform sauce.
3. Season with the garlic powder, nutmeg, nutritional yeast, ½ teaspoon salt and a pinch of pepper.
4. Continue mixing the sauce until it reaches a thick, creamy consistency.

To prepare the cashew cream:

1. In a small pot, place the raw cashews with 1½ cups water and bring to a boil. Let boil for 10 minutes, then remove from the stove and cool down.
2. Add the entire contents of the pot to a blender, and blend with the rest of the cashew cream ingredients until you get a smooth sauce.

To prepare the creamy cauliflower casserole:

1. Preheat the oven to 425°F.
2. Combine the cauliflower mash with the cheesy sauce and the cashew cream.
3. Pour the mix in a baking dish. Bake for 60 minutes or until golden on top. Serve warm.

Printed in Great Britain
by Amazon